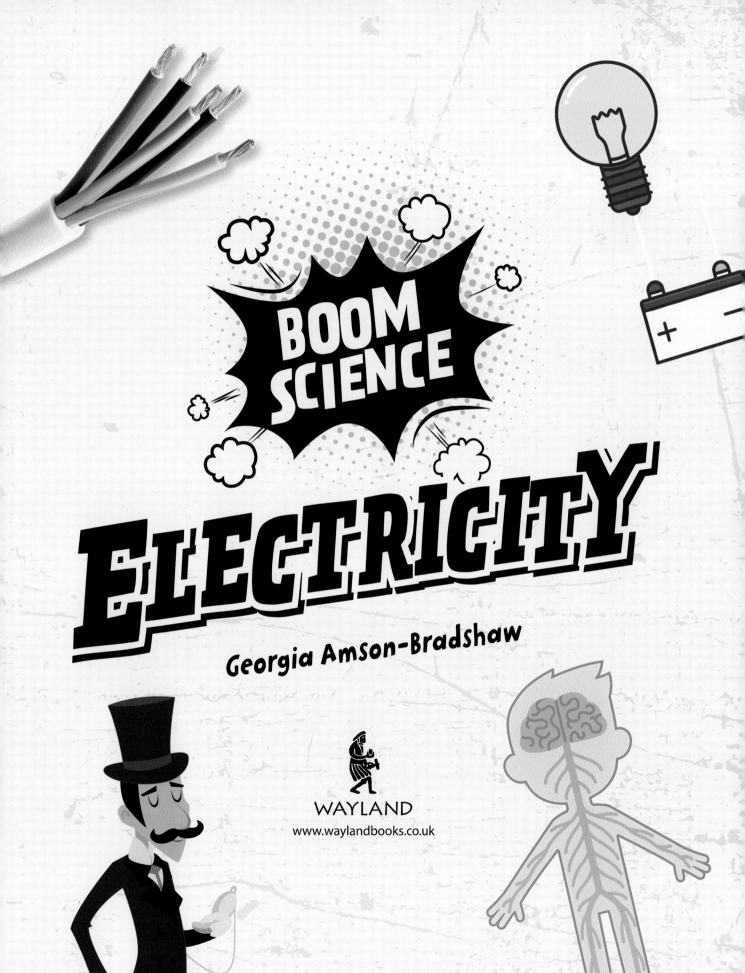

BOOM SCIENCE

ELECTRICITY

Georgia Amson-Bradshaw

WAYLAND
www.waylandbooks.co.uk

Published in paperback in Great Britain in 2019 by Wayland

Copyright © Hodder and Stoughton Limited, 2018

Produced for Wayland by
White-Thomson Publishing Ltd
www.wtpub.co.uk

All rights reserved.

Series Editor: Georgia Amson-Bradshaw
Series Designer: Rocket Design (East Anglia) Ltd

ISBN: 978 1 5263 0657 9
10 9 8 7 6 5 4 3 2 1

Wayland
An imprint of
Hachette Children's Group
Part of Hodder & Stoughton
Carmelite House
50 Victoria Embankment
London EC4Y 0DZ

An Hachette UK Company
www.hachette.co.uk
www.hachettechildrens.co.uk

Printed in China

Picture acknowledgements:
Images from Shutterstock.com: Visual Generation 6t, Igor Lateci 6b, jwls1914 6b,
Volodymyr Krasyuk 6b, Happy Stock Photo 6b, Dmitrydesign 7t, Meilun 7b, NotionPic 8,
J R Patterson 9t, Sudowoodo 10t, wildestanimal 10b, Phanuwat_Nandee 11t, Dark Moon Pictures 11b,
Dino Osmic 14b, KorradolYamsatthm 15b, haryigit 16b, Monkey Business Images 17b, Smileus 18t,
Africa Studio 19b, NadyaArt 19t, Nucleartist 22t, ULKASTUDIO 23t, Yury Kosourov 23c, ankomando 23b,
Georgii Red 26t, Sentavio 26b, Georgii Red 27t, OxfordSquare 27b

All illustrations on pages 12, 13, 20, 21, 24, 25 by Steve Evans

All design elements from Shutterstock.

Every effort has been made to clear copyright. Should there
be any inadvertent omission, please apply to the publisher
for rectification.

The website addresses (URLs) included in this book were
valid at the time of going to press. However, it is possible that
contents or addresses may have changed since the publication
of this book. No responsibility for any such changes can be
accepted by either the author or the publisher.

WARNING! ELECTRICITY IS DANGEROUS!

Never play with electrical objects.
Do not put anything into plug sockets
in the wall. Always ask an adult for
help with any experiments.

Glossary words are shown in bold.

CONTENTS

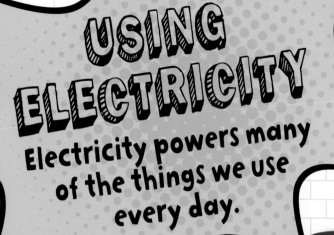

USING ELECTRICITY

Electricity powers many of the things we use every day.

ALL AROUND US

Think about breakfast time. Do you ever eat toast from a toaster? Drink juice or milk from the fridge? Is the radio on while you eat? All of these **devices** are powered by electricity.

HEY, WHAT AM I?

Two of these objects use electricity to work, and two don't. Which are they? Answer on page 28.

computer

washing machine

toilet · acoustic guitar

ELECTRICAL WORLD

Electricity powers the machines in the factories where our things are made. It powers the Internet and telephone networks. Many trains run on electricity. Without electricity, our lives would be very different!

WOW!

Scientists such as Benjamin Franklin were experimenting with electricity in the eighteenth century, but it wasn't until the late nineteenth century that electric lighting was used in city street lights.

WHAT IS ELECTRICITY?

Electricity is a type of energy.

PROVIDING POWER

Energy is what makes things happen. Electricity is one type, but there are lots of different types of energy. Electricity can be turned into different types of useful energy by our devices.

I'm hot stuff!

An iron turns electrical energy into heat energy.

I'm the brightest.

A fan turns electrical energy into movement energy, spinning the fan blades.

I've got the best moves!

A light bulb turns electrical energy into light energy.

CARRYING ENERGY

We move electricity from place to place through metal wires. Thick **cables** carry electricity from **power stations** to towns and cities, where electricity is needed. Tall **pylons** hold the cables safely up in the air.

PLUG AND GO

Inside our homes, we plug our devices into **sockets** in the wall to get electricity that has travelled from power stations. Some devices use more electrical energy than others. For example a tumble dryer uses ten times as much energy as a fridge-freezer.

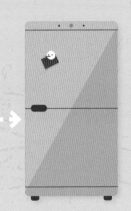

ELECTRICITY IN NATURE

Electricity occurs naturally, as well as being man-made.

brain

nerves

BUZZING BRAIN

Electricity doesn't just come out of the sockets in the wall. In fact, it's inside you right now! Our bodies use electricity to send information between our brains and the rest of our bodies along our **nerves**.

HEY, WHAT AM I?

Some animals are able to sense the electricity inside other living things, helping them hunt for prey. Which expert electricity hunter can you see in this picture?
Answer on page 28.

STATIC CRACKLE

Have you ever touched an object and felt a little spark? That is **static electricity**. Unlike the electricity that powers our devices, it doesn't flow through wires. Instead, it builds up in one place, then is released in a single spark.

ZZZAP!

Zoinks!

SHOCKING STORMS

Lightning is a bolt of natural electricity from the sky. It happens during thunderstorms. It is actually a hugely powerful spark of static electricity that jumps from the clouds to the ground.

YOUR TURN!

MAKE STATIC SPARKS

See how static electricity builds up and is then released with a spark in this experiment. You'll need:

A piece of woollen fabric

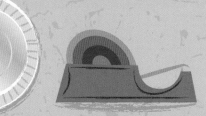

A polystyrene cup

A polystyrene block (or plate)

Aluminium pie dish

A roll of sticky tape

STEP ONE

Tape the cup upside down in the middle of the pie dish, and set aside.

STEP TWO

Rub the polystyrene block (or plate, placed upside down) with the wool for one minute.

STEP THREE

Holding the polystyrene cup, place the pie dish on top of the polystyrene block, in the centre. Very quickly touch the metal of the pie dish. Do you feel a spark?

STEP FOUR

Lift the pie dish into the air using the cup as a handle. Touch the dish again with your other hand. Do you feel a spark? How many times can you place the pie dish on the polystyrene block without rubbing it again, and still get a spark when you touch it?

CIRCUITS AND CURRENTS

Electricity needs to flow in a loop to keep working.

ROUND AND AROUND

Our devices are powered by **electrical currents**. Unlike static electricity, this sort of electricity flows around and around – as long as there is a **circuit** for it to flow around.

CIRCUIT INGREDIENTS

For an electrical current to flow, a circuit needs a power source, such as a **battery**, and wires to carry the electricity around in a loop.

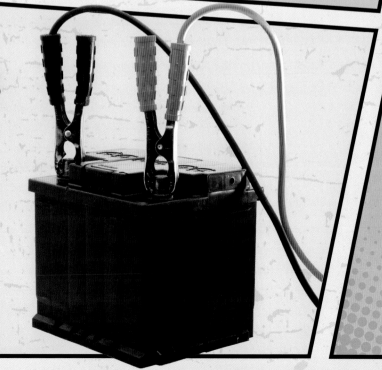

POWERING DEVICES

You can add a **component**, such as a light bulb, to a circuit and the electricity will flow through it, making it work.

HIDE AND SEEK

Can you spot a light bulb that does NOT have electricity flowing through it? Answer on page 28.

WOW!

The circuits inside some of our devices are very complicated. Electrical engineers who design devices draw diagrams to help them keep track of all the wires and components.

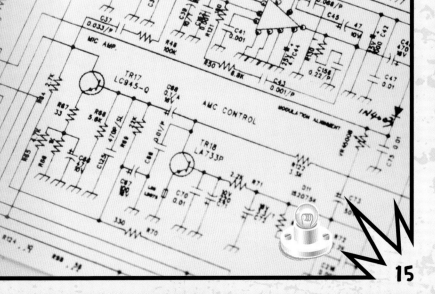

SWITCHES

A switch makes a break in a circuit to stop electricity flowing.

Oh no, I can't get around!

BROKEN CIRCUIT

If there is a gap or a break in the circuit, the electrical current stops flowing.

ON AND OFF

We don't want all of our devices to be switched on and working all the time, so we put breaks in the circuits that can stop the electricity flowing. These are called switches.

a simple circuit

← - - - switch

battery

← - - - bulb

SIMPLE SWITCH

A switch like this one works because it is made of metal, like the wires. When the switch is closed, all the metal is touching, making a complete loop. When the switch is lifted open, it makes a gap in the circuit, stopping the electricity from flowing around.

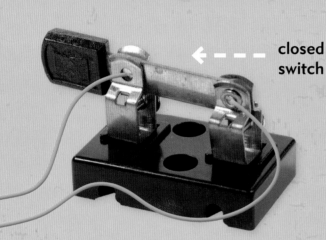

closed switch

open switch

HEY, WHAT AM I?

What sort of switch can you see in this picture? How do you think it works?
Answer on page 28.

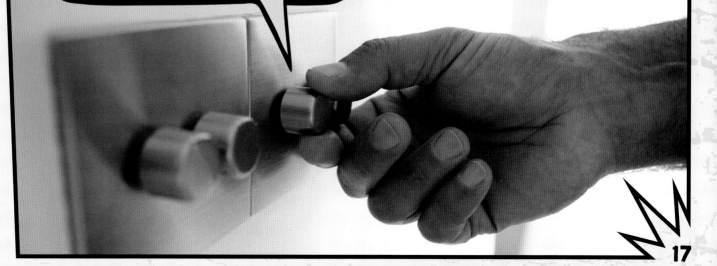

BATTERIES

A battery is used to store chemical energy.

PORTABLE ENERGY

We can't always plug our devices into a socket to get electricity. Sometimes we need power on the move. This is when batteries are useful.

POSITIVE AND NEGATIVE

Batteries have a positive and a negative end. When connected to a circuit containing a device, electricity flows from the negative end to the positive end, powering the device along the way.

This is my positive end!

This is my negative end ...

ENERGY STORE

Batteries contain chemicals. Batteries work by turning energy from these chemicals into electrical energy that powers a device. It's a bit like how when you eat, you turn **chemical energy** from food into the energy you use to make your body work. But the chemicals in batteries are different and you should never eat a battery!

ARGH! NO! Batteries contain dangerous chemicals!

If I eat this battery, will it give me electrical energy?

HIDE AND SEEK

Like sweets, batteries contain energy and come in all shapes and sizes. Can you spot three different types hiding? Answer on page 29.

MAKE A BATTERY

See how chemical energy is turned into electrical energy with this fruity experiment. You'll need:

Four **galvanised** nails

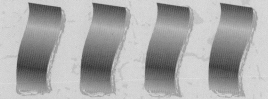

Four lemons

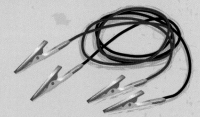

A light emitting diode (LED)

Five alligator clip wires

Four pieces of copper

STEP ONE

Release the juice inside the lemons by rolling and squeezing them until they feel softer. Then, insert one nail and one piece of copper into each lemon. You might need an adult to help you cut a slit for the copper.

STEP TWO

Connect the lemons using the clip wires, going from nail to copper piece. Once you have connected the four lemons you should have one nail and one piece of copper not yet attached.

STEP THREE

Using the last two wires, connect the spare copper piece to the positive (long) end of the LED. Connect the spare nail to the negative (short) end of the LED. This completes the circuit, and the LED should light up.

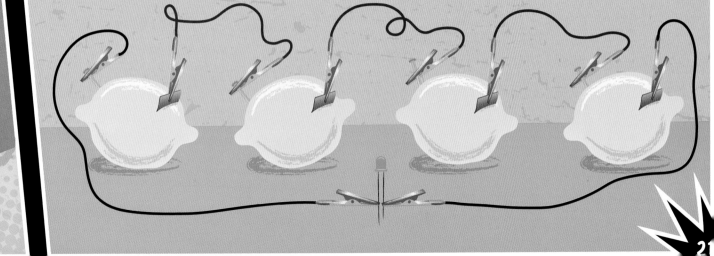

ELECTRICITY AND MATERIALS

Electricity flows through some materials, but not others.

CONDUCTORS

Materials such as metals or water let electricity flow through them. We call these materials **conductors**.

WOO HOO! I can flow through this water!

INSULATORS

Materials such as plastic and wood do not let electricity flow through them. These are **insulators**. Because electricity is dangerous, we use a mixture of conductors and insulators in our devices.

Oh no, I can't go through plastic.

STAYING SAFE

The wires that connect our devices to the electricity supply are metal on the inside, but are coated in plastic. This lets electricity travel easily to the device, but stops us from getting an **electric shock** if we touch them.

HEY, WHAT AM I?

Most wires are made of this type of metal. Do you know what it is? Answer on page 29.

WOW!

Humans are 70 per cent water, so we conduct electricity! However, it's very dangerous. If a powerful electrical current flows through you, it can cause serious injuries or death.

YOUR TURN!

WHAT CONDUCTS ELECTRICITY?

Test which materials let electricity flow through them in this experiment. You'll need:

A 1.5 volt bulb in a holder

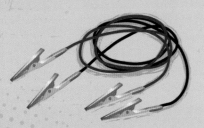

Three alligator clip wires

An AA battery in a holder

A selection of objects such as a metal key, a plastic peg, a rubber, a teaspoon, a paper clip

STEP ONE

Connect the bulb to the battery using the first wire. Connect the second wire to the other end of the battery, and the third wire to the other side of the bulb, creating a broken circuit. Touch the free ends of the wires together to check the bulb lights up when the circuit is completed.

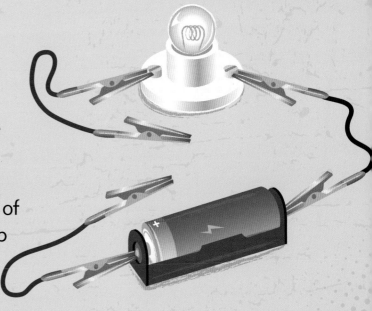

STEP TWO

One at a time, connect the objects to the circuit using the free clips, and check if the bulb lights up. The bulb will light up if the connected object does conduct electricity.

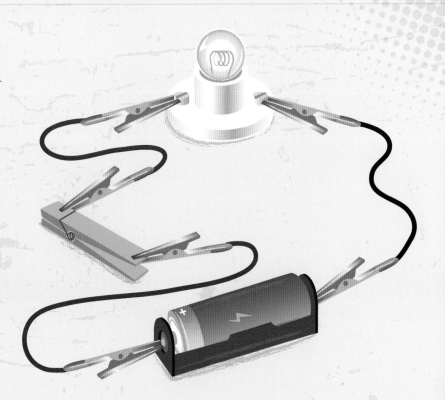

STEP THREE

Test each of the objects in turn and group them together according to whether they conduct electricity or not. Look at your two piles. What do you notice about the objects that do conduct electricity? Answer on page 29.

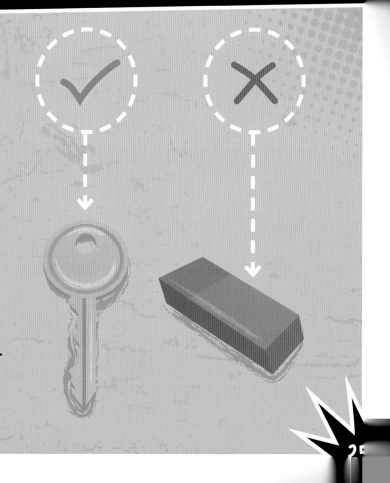

MAKING ELECTRICITY

Different types of energy are changed into electricity.

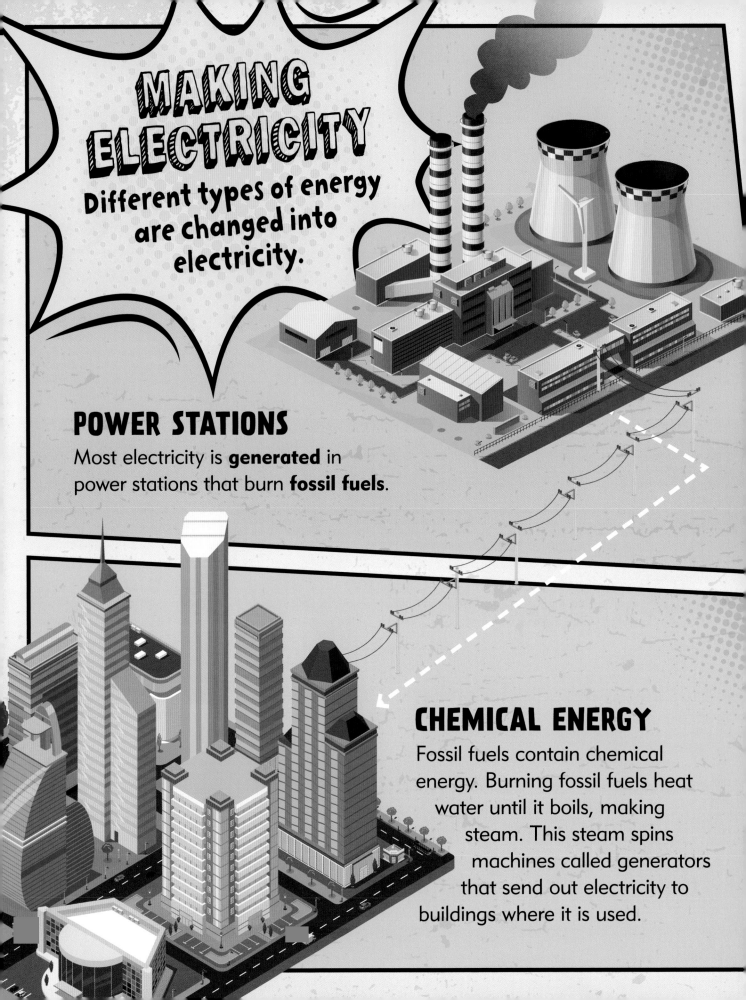

POWER STATIONS

Most electricity is **generated** in power stations that burn **fossil fuels**.

CHEMICAL ENERGY

Fossil fuels contain chemical energy. Burning fossil fuels heat water until it boils, making steam. This steam spins machines called generators that send out electricity to buildings where it is used.

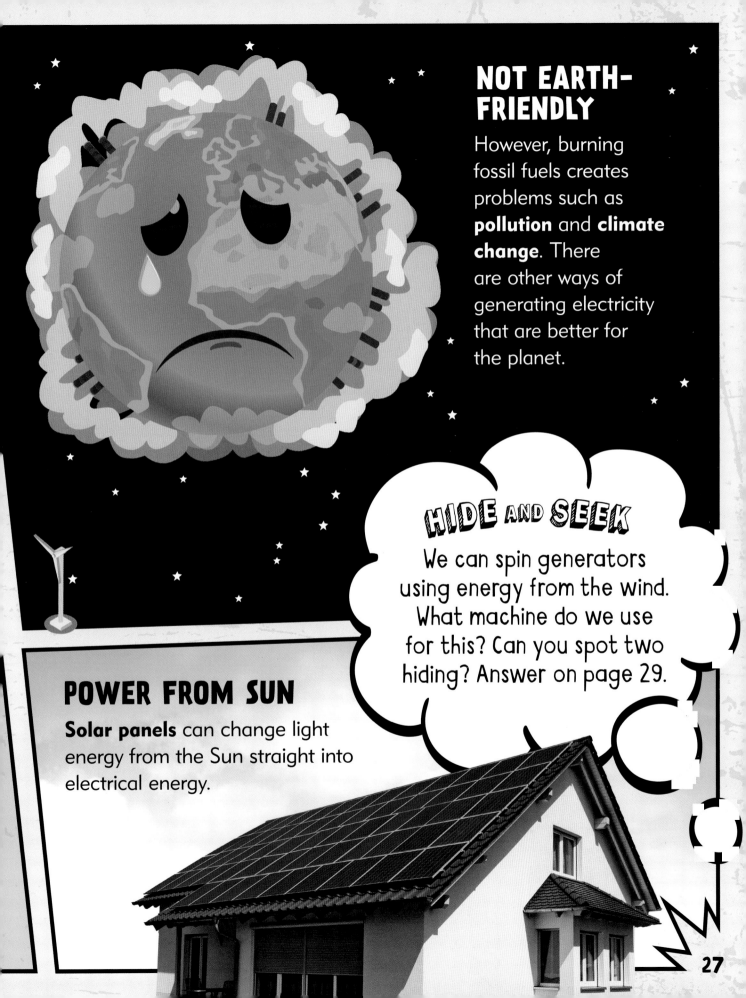

NOT EARTH-FRIENDLY

However, burning fossil fuels creates problems such as **pollution** and **climate change**. There are other ways of generating electricity that are better for the planet.

HIDE AND SEEK

We can spin generators using energy from the wind. What machine do we use for this? Can you spot two hiding? Answer on page 29.

POWER FROM SUN

Solar panels can change light energy from the Sun straight into electrical energy.

ANSWERS

Page 6

What am I? Toilets and acoustic guitars don't use electricity to work.

Page 10

What am I? I'm a shark.

Page 15

Hide and Seek
Light bulb

CIRCUITS AND CURRENTS

I love to loop the loop!

Electricity needs to flow in a loop to keep working.

ROUND AND AROUND
Our devices are powered by **electrical currents**. Unlike static electricity, this sort of electricity flows around and around – as long as there is a **circuit** for it to flow around.

CIRCUIT INGREDIENTS
For an electrical current to flow, a circuit needs a power source, such as a battery, and wires to carry the electricity around in a loop.

POWERING DEVICES
You can add a **component**, such as a light bulb to a circuit, and the electricity will flow through it, making it work.

HIDE AND SEEK
Can you spot a light bulb that does NOT have electricity flowing through it? Answer on page 29.

WOW!
The circuits inside some of our devices are very complicated. Electrical engineers who design devices draw diagrams to help them keep track of all the wires and components.

14   15

Page 17

What am I? The switch in the picture is a dimmer switch on a light. Instead of just breaking the circuit, it changes the amount of electricity flowing through the bulb, making it brighter or dimmer.

8

Page 19

Hide and Seek Batteries: 9 volt battery, watch battery and AA battery

Page 23

What am I? I'm copper. Copper is a type of metal that conducts electricity very well.

Page 25

Your turn Once you've tested quite a few objects, you'll probably notice that the ones that conduct electricity are made of metal. Objects made of wood, plastic, cloth or rubber do not conduct electricity.

Page 27

Hide and Seek Wind turbines

GLOSSARY

battery an object that stores energy and can power electrical devices

cable a thick rope made of metal wires twisted together that can carry electricity

chemical energy a type of energy that is contained in chemicals

circuit a closed loop that electricity can flow around

climate change changes in weather around the world caused by human activity

component one part of an electrical circuit or device

conductor a material that lets electricity pass through it

device an object that works using electricity

electric shock a sudden flow of electricity through the body

electrical current electricity that is flowing around a circuit

energy what makes things move and work

fossil fuel materials that are burned to power machines

galvanise to cover with a layer of zinc, which is a type of metal

generate to make something, such as electricity

insulator a material that does not let electricity pass through it

nerve something in the body that carries information between the brain and other body parts

pollution when the air, water or land is made dirty by waste or harmful chemicals

power station a place where electricity is generated before being carried to homes and cities

pylon large metal structures that hold electrical cables high in the air, safe from people

socket a hole in the wall into which devices can be plugged to get electricity

solar panel a device that can turn light energy from sunshine into electricity

static electricity a type of electricity that builds up in one place and doesn't flow around a circuit

INDEX

Boom Science Series contents lists